Pebble Bilingual Books

El agua como gas/
Water as a Gas

de/by
Helen Frost

Traducción/Translation
Martín Luis Guzmán Ferrer, Ph.D.

Capstone Press
Mankato, Minnesota

Pebble Bilingual Books are published by Capstone Press
151 Good Counsel Drive, P.O. Box 669, Mankato, Minnesota 56002
http://www.capstone-press.com

1 2 3 4 5 6 08 07 06 05 04 03

Library of Congress Cataloging-in-Publication Data
Frost, Helen, 1949–
[Water as a gas. Spanish & English.]
El agua como gas / de Helen Frost; traducción, Martín Luis Guzmán Ferrer = Water as a gas /
by Helen Frost; translation, Martín Luis Guzmán Ferrerr.
p. cm.—(Pebble Bilingual Books)
Text in Spanish and English.
Summary: Simple text presents facts about the properties and behavior of water in the state of
a gas.
ISBN 0-7368-2311-5 (hardcover)
1. Water vapor, Atmospheric—Juvenile literature. [1. Steam. 2. Water vapor, Atmospheric.
3. Water. 4. Spanish language materials—Bilingual.] I. Title: Water as a gas. II. Title.
QC915 .F7618 2004
531.57—dc21   2002156344

Editorial Credits
Mari C. Schuh and Martha E. H. Rustad, editors; Timothy Halldin, cover designer; Linda Clavel,
interior designer; Patrick Dentinger, cover production designer; Kimberly Danger, photo
researcher; María Fiol, Spanish copy editor; Gail Saunders-Smith, consulting editor; Carolyn
M. Tucker, Water Education Specialist, California Department of Water Resources, reviewer

Photo Credits
David F. Clobes, cover, 20; Diane Meyer, 18; Jack Glisson, 4; James P. Rowan, 1; Kate Boykin, 12;
Photri-Microstock, 6, 14; Richard B. Levine, 16; Unicorn Stock Photos/Jean Higgins, 8; Visuals
Unlimited, 10

Special thanks to:
• Isabel Schon, Ph.D., director of the Barahona Center for the Study of Books in Spanish for
  Children and Adolescents, San Marcos, California, for her assistance in preparing the Spanish
  portion of this book.
• Dr. Josué Njock Libii of Purdue University-Fort Wayne in Fort Wayne, Indiana, for his helpful
  assistance with the English portion of this book.

Table of Contents

Water Vapor 5
Evaporation 7
Condensation. 13
Steam 19
Glossary. 22
Index 24

Contenido

El agua como gas 5
La evaporación 7
La condensación. 13
El vapor 19
Glosario. 23
Índice 24

Water can be a solid,
a liquid, or a gas.
Water as a gas is called
water vapor. You cannot
see water vapor.

El agua puede ser sólido,
líquido o gas. El agua
como gas se llama
vapor de agua. Tú no
puedes ver el vapor de agua.

Heat changes water from a liquid into a vapor. The sun heats water. Water vapor rises into the air. This action is evaporation.

El calor cambia el agua de líquido a vapor. El sol calienta el agua. El vapor de agua sube al aire. Esto se llama evaporación.

8

Evaporation makes
wet things dry. Wet
clothes dry in the sun.

La evaporación seca
las cosas mojadas. La ropa
mojada se seca al sol.

More heat makes water
evaporate fast. Puddles
dry up fast on hot days.

Si hace más calor, el agua
se evapora más rápido. Los
charcos se secan rápidamente
en días calurosos.

Water vapor turns into a liquid when it cools. This action is condensation.

El vapor de agua se convierte en líquido cuando se enfría. Esto se llama condensación.

14

Condensation can form
clouds. Clouds are dust
and tiny drops of water.

La condensación puede formar
nubes. Las nubes son de
polvo y de gotitas de agua.

Humid air holds a lot
of water vapor. Humid
air feels wet.

El aire húmedo contiene
mucho vapor de agua. El aire
húmedo se siente mojado.

Boiling water makes steam. Steam is water vapor mixed with tiny drops of water.

Cuando el agua hierve se hace vapor. El vapor se mezcla con gotitas de agua.

People use steam
to iron clothes.

Las personas usan vapor
para planchar la ropa.

Glossary

boil—to heat water or another liquid until it starts to bubble; water boils when it reaches 212 degrees Fahrenheit (100 degrees Celsius); water gives off steam when it boils.

condense—to change from a gas into a liquid

evaporate—to change from a liquid into a gas

gas—a substance, such as air, that spreads to fill any space that holds it; water as a gas is called water vapor.

humid—damp and moist; humid air holds a lot of water vapor.

liquid—a substance that flows freely; water as a liquid fills oceans, lakes, and rivers.

solid—something that holds its shape; ice and snow are examples of water as a solid.

Glosario

hervir—calentar agua o otro líquido hasta que burbujea; el agua hierve cuando alcanza 100 grados Celsius (212 grados Fahrenheit); del agua sale vapor cuando hierve.

condensar—cambiar de gas a líquido

evaporar—cambiar de líquido a gas

gas *(el)*—una sustancia, como el aire, que se extiende hasta llenar el espacio que la contiene; el agua como gas se llama vapor de agua.

húmedo—mojado, lluvioso; el aire húmedo tiene mucho vapor de agua.

líquido *(el)*—una sustancia que corre libremente; el agua como líquido llena los mares, los lagos y los ríos.

sólido *(el)*—algo que guarda su forma; el hielo y la nieve son ejemplos del agua como sólido.

Index

air, 7, 17
boiling, 19
clothes, 9, 21
clouds, 15
condensation,
   13, 15
cools, 13
drops, 15, 19
dry, 9, 11

dust, 15
evaporation, 7, 9
form, 15
gas, 5
heat, 7, 11
humid, 17
iron, 21
liquid, 5, 7, 13
puddles, 11

solid, 5
steam, 19, 21
sun, 7, 9
vapor, 7
water, 5, 7, 11,
   15, 19
water vapor, 5,
   7, 13, 17, 19
wet, 9, 17

Índice

agua, 5, 7, 11,
   15, 19
aire, 7, 17
calor, 7, 11
calurosos, 11
condensación,
   13, 15
charcos, 11
enfría, 13
evaporación,
   7, 9

formar, 15
gas, 5
gotitas, 15, 19
hierve, 19
húmedo, 17
líquido, 5, 7, 13
mojado, 9, 17
nubes, 15
planchar, 21
polvo, 15
ropa, 9, 21

secar, 9
sol, 7, 9
sólido, 5
vapor, 7,
   19, 21
vapor de agua,
   5, 7, 13, 17